MY PET HAMSTER

written by **Lyn Thomas**

illustrated by **Jane Kurisu**

Kids Can Press

Hamsters Are Us!

Hi. My name is Tumbleweed. Hamsters are the cutest, most awesome animals in the world, and I am one! So in this book I can tell you how to take care of your own hamster.

You'll also find places in this book just for you to write about you and your hamster. Look for the hamster notebook section like this one.

My Hamster Notebook

My name is _____.

I am _____ years old.   I am a ◯ girl   ◯ boy.

I got this book because

◯ I want to get a hamster

◯ I already have a hamster

◯ I want to know more about hamsters

◯ _____

Rodent Roundup

Did you know that hamsters are rodents? You can tell because we have two big front teeth.

Hamster Habits

All rodents are cool, but hamsters rule! Here are some things you should know about hamsters:

- We love playing, especially at night.
- We carry our food in our cheek pouches and sometimes hide it for later.
- We love digging. In the wild, we build tunnels underground.

Tumbleweed Tip

Like all rodents, I have front teeth that keep growing all my life. To keep them from getting too long, I have to chew! Give your pet hamster something good to chew on, such as a small apple branch. Make sure the wood is not treated with chemicals.

Try this! Here are some other rodents. Compare them with the drawing of gorgeous me. What are some of the ways that I look different from the other rodents? Circle the parts of the mouse, gerbil, guinea pig and beaver that are different from mine.

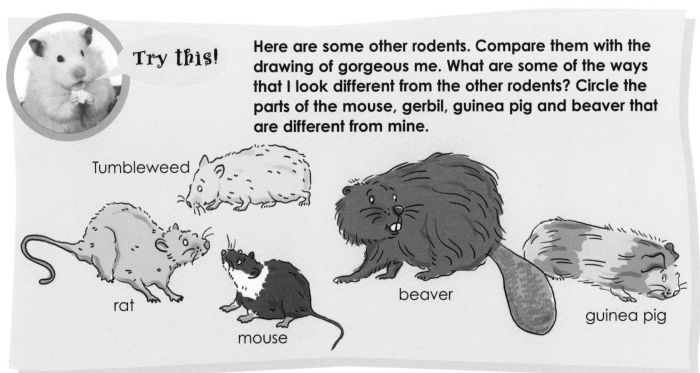

Tumbleweed

rat

mouse

beaver

guinea pig

Choosing a Great Pet

Most hamsters you see are golden Syrian hamsters, with beautiful golden fur like mine. But hamsters come in many colors. We can be multicolored, spotted, longhaired, fluffy — just about anything. Well, maybe not plaid or green!

Getting a Healthy, Happy Hamster

If you're looking for a hamster to take home, make sure you get one as awesome as I am — or almost.

● Choose the liveliest, most alert hamster in the litter.

● Do you want a male or a female hamster? The person at the pet store can help you decide.

● If you want more than one hamster, check with the pet store about what kind to get. Some of us don't like roommates and will fight!

● Your hamster should have shiny eyes and be clean around the ears and near the tail. And make sure it has shiny, thick fur — like mine!

My Hamster Notebook

I will be a good hamster owner. I can check off as true most or all of the points below, so I know my pet hamster and I will be happy together.

- ⭘ I keep my room clean (well, most of the time).

- ⭘ No one at home gets sick from animal fur.

- ⭘ If I have other pets, I can make sure that my hamster is always safe from them.

- ⭘ I will take care of my pet every day, or have someone do it for me if I can't.

- ⭘ I am prepared to buy or grow good food for my pet.

I will call my hamster _____

because _____ .

Tumbleweed Trivia
How is a baby hamster like a baby dog?
Answer: They are both called puppies.

Hamster Home

We hamsters are only little, but we still like clean, large homes. We need lots of room to play, exercise, make nests, store our food and have a tidy toilet area.

Home, Sweet Hamster Home

Find the perfect spot in a room for a hamster home. I like a home that is

● away from drafty windows and doors

● not up against a radiator, over an air vent, close to a heater or fire, or in direct sunlight. I don't like it too hot!

● above floor level — such as on a stool or table

● in a spot where the noise I make won't be heard at night. I don't want to keep you awake!

The Coolest Cage

What kind of cage are you going to buy? Here are some of the kinds you can get:

● Fish tanks are fun. You can see in, and we can see what's going on outside! You'll need a screen on top, to keep your hamster from getting out and let enough air in.

● Wire cages are great, as we love to climb walls! But the kind with grates at the bottom are hard to clean and can hurt little hamster feet.

● Plastic cages with lots of tunnels and rooms are great for playing. But the plastic must be very strong, or we can chew through it.

Horrible Hamster Homes

No, these aren't places where bad hamsters live! Some things don't make good hamster homes, such as boxes made of cardboard, wood and some plastics, because

- your hamster would easily chew his way out of wood or cardboard
- not enough light would get in, and hamsters need light
- a wood or cardboard box would get damp, making it a place for germs to grow
- some plastics contain substances that are poisonous to your hamster

Try this!

Make a fabulous, Tumbleweed-approved Burrowing Hamsterquarium! Put a fairly heavy metal or plastic cage on top of a fish tank. Fill the fish tank with peat, hay and wood shavings for burrowing. Don't forget to make a ramp down from the top cage into the bottom.

Welcome Home, Hamster!

When I was taken to a new home, everything was ready for me. It made me feel really special and at home nearly right away.

Hamster Have-to-haves

Now that you have a great cage for your hamster to live in, you'll need
- a toilet tray and rodent litter (don't use cat litter)
- non-tipping ceramic food bowls
- a water bottle attached to the side of the cage
- a sleeping box and nesting material

My Hamster Notebook

When I brought it home, the first thing my pet hamster did was

○ build a nest   ○ use its toilet tray

○ play   ○ sleep

○ hide   ○ _____

Happy Homecoming

When you get your hamster home, let it into the cage you have ready for it — home sweet home! Remove the nesting material from the carrying box and put it into the new cage along with the new nesting material. The first thing I did was explore my new world and make my home all mine. Your hamster will need to do the same, and mark its new home with its scent glands.

Homecoming No-nos

These are things you should not do after you bring your hamster home:

● Don't move things around in the cage for a few days — your hamster will need time to get used to where everything is.
● Don't play with your hamster for a few days — peace and quiet is best for a while.

Tumbleweed Tip

Most hamsters hate loud sound.
Try not to disturb us with strange noises — or we'll call the hamster police with a noise complaint!

Hamster's First Day

Now you've got your hamster home and it's settling in. At first, you have to take it slow!

Getting to Know You

Your hamster will probably be shy. Quietly hold your hand up to the cage. Talk to your hamster and let it sniff your fingers. Offer it a little treat, such as a piece of apple or a seed. It'll try a grab-and-run, but don't let it! Hold on to the food and let the hamster nibble away. Once the hamster is eating, you can begin to gently rub its back. Don't rub too fast or from behind where it can't see you.

How Heavy?

To weigh your hamster, put a paper towel in the measuring container of a small weighing scale and place your hamster in it. You will have to be very quick, because hamsters move fast!

How Long?

Once your hamster is used to you, make sure it is fully awake and let it sniff your hand before you lift it. Have a parent take a soft tape measure and place it over your hamster from the tip of its nose along its back to its tail.

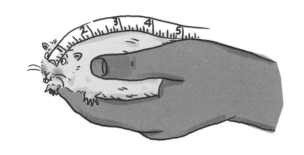

My Hamster Notebook

This is what my hamster is like now, on its first day home.

Date: _____ My hamster's name: _____

Length: _____ Weight: _____

Age (ask at the pet store): _____

Color: _____ ○ Male or ○ Female

An interesting thing I've noticed about my hamster:

_____

My hamster is one-of-a-kind!
This is what my hamster looks like.
(Color this illustration to match your hamster.)

Tumbleweed Trivia
You love your hamster,
but you should not kiss it. Why?
Answer: Because you can spread
germs to each other.

Seeds and So Much More

Here's my favorite part — all about food!

Hamster Mealtime

Most hamsters should eat about 14 grams, or one tablespoon, of food each day. Hamsters need to drink a lot of water, especially those who eat dry food.

I like regular mealtimes and so will your hamster. Feed your hamster at the same time each day.

Pet stores will have seeds, grain pellets and food mixes especially for hamsters — they know what I like! They also have patties made out of seeds — like nutty hamburgers! And don't forget the fresh fruits and vegetables.

Tumbleweed Tip
Don't give your hamster too much lettuce, as it can cause an upset tummy. I like small salads, not big ones!

My Hamster Notebook

I give my hamster lots of different things to eat. Here are my hamster's favorites (circle the pictures):

processed wheat or oats

dog biscuits

celery

ground nut pellets

grapes

peas

lettuce

broccoli

vitamins and minerals

sunflower seeds

carrot

corn cob

strawberries

Hints for Hamster Feeding

- Put dry food in a sturdy bowl made of ceramic or non-toxic plastic.
- Keep the water bottle away from the food bowl. If water drips into the food, it will go bad.
- Don't buy too much food at once, or it will go bad or stale.
- Always wash fruits and vegetables, even if they look clean.

A Happy Hamster Day

Your hamster and its home need everyday care to keep clean. I'm a happy hamster because my owners make sure that
- I am fed at the same time every day
- my food bowls are washed and my water changed
- my food stash doesn't have anything yucky in it
- my litter is clean
- I'm looking good. If I were longhaired, I'd need grooming. But I'm just naturally beautiful!

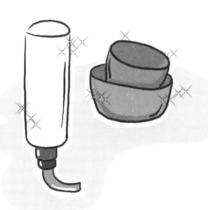

Tumbleweed Trivia

Hamsters are omnivores. What does that mean?
Answer: It means we eat plants and also other animals. In the wild, we would eat seeds, plants, insects, worms and sometimes mice.

My Hamster Notebook

I watch my hamster and play with it every day. These are some things I've noticed about my pet.

Does it like to eat at the same time every day?

○ No   ○ Yes   When? _____

Its favorite treat is _____.

Does it like to hide food?

○ Yes   ○ No

Its special place to hide its food is _____.

My hamster sleeps _____ hours each day.

I do these other things for my hamster each day:

○ I talk to it, and I say, _____.

○ I take it out of its cage and hold it.

○ _____

Hamster Health

Your hamster can't tell you if it's feeling sick, and neither can I. So how can you tell if your hamster is healthy? Here are some things to look for:

Signs of Problems	Possible Causes
Bare spots	Bad diet
Weight Loss	Not enough food
Thin smelly stools	Bad food; too much corn; damp cage; too cold
Scratching and red skin	Cage not clean; not enough grooming; infection
Sneezing	Temperature imbalance; cage near a draft
Teeth or nails too long	Not able to climb or dig enough
Not eating	Temperature imbalance
Doesn't like light	Eye infection from draft or dusty litter

Weekly Work

These are things you should do at least once a week to keep your hamster as happy and healthy as me!

● Wash the cage with dishwashing liquid and water, wipe it with disinfectant and dry with a clean towel.

● Use a bottle brush to scrub out the inside of your hamster's water bottle.

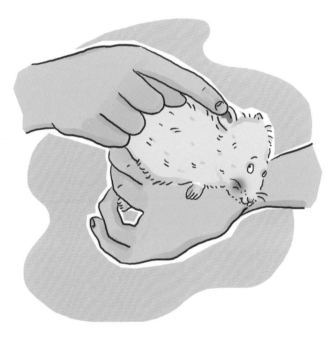

● Change the bedding and nesting materials.

● Weigh your hamster.

● Check its ears by pulling back each earflap very gently. They should be clean and not smelly.

● Check to make sure your hamster's eyes are clear, shiny and bright.

● If you have a longhaired hamster, untangle knots and remove anything caught in its fur.

Tumbleweed Trivia

Do you have to bathe your hamster?
Answer: No, mostly we do a great job of grooming ourselves! We use our tongues, paws, teeth and claws to keep ourselves shiny and beautiful. You should brush or comb longhaired hamsters.

Hamster Talk

Have fun watching your pet! Hamsters are really smart, but your hamster can't talk to you in your language. So it has to show you what it means in other ways. Look closely, and soon your hamster's messages will start coming through loud and clear!

Be a Body Detective

You don't have to be Hamster Holmes to solve this mystery. Do you know what your hamster is doing or saying when it does certain things?

What hamster is doing	What hamster is saying
Looking tense and shivering	Something is wrong.
Lying on back with mouth open and teeth showing	I'm frightened.
Sitting upright with paws hanging in front	Oh boy, I feel relaxed.
Peeping out of nesting place	Is everything safe out there?
Ears are lying back	I'm in a bit of a bad mood.
Leaping in the air	Life is fun, I'm really happy!
Fills up its cheeks and looking alert	I see an enemy, so if I look big I can scare it away!

My Hamster Notebook

I feel like I know my hamster so well that it's almost like we talk to each other.

My hamster understands me when I say these things:

_____

_____

These are things my hamster does to let me know it likes me:

_____

My hamster

○ likes music

○ sleeps a lot

○ leaps around and has fun

○ _____

Tumbleweed Tip
Don't share your chocolate treats with your hamster. Chocolate might be yummy for you, but it's poisonous to me.

Having Hamster Fun

Hamsters are very active and way too smart to like being bored. So we make every day a play day!

My Hamster Notebook

I love watching my pet hamster play!

I notice my hamster

○ sniffs new things

○ loves to leap

○ runs really fast

○ _____

My hamster's favorite toy is _____.

The best game my hamster and I play is _____.

Tumbleweed Trivia

Who hears better, you or your hamster?
Answer: Your hamster and I can hear much better than you. That's why your hamster will very quickly learn to know your voice from other people's voices.

Out and About

If you let your hamster out of its cage to have fun, make sure it is in an enclosed space and that the room is hamster safe. Make sure that

- all heating vents are covered — we can get into them sometimes!
- windows and doors are closed — we can escape pretty quickly
- electrical cords are out of the way — chewing these is dangerous

Try this!

Make a hamster play maze

1. Cut hamster-sized holes in shoe boxes. Connect the boxes to form a maze.

2. Connect the boxes with cardboard rolls from paper towels, wrapping paper or toilet paper.

3. Use PVC plastic pipes for your hamster to run through between boxes.

4. Old socks with the toe-end cut off make cool soft tunnels for hamsters to burrow in and out of.

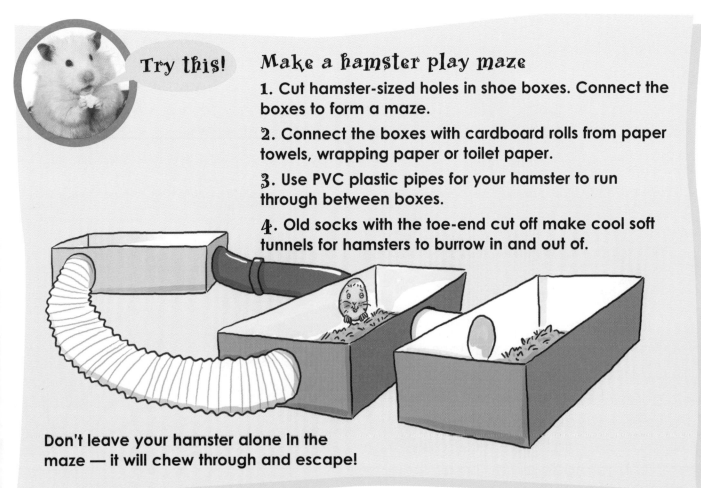

Don't leave your hamster alone in the maze — it will chew through and escape!

Tumbleweed Tale

One of the best things about hamsters is the amazing but true stories about us. Here's one of my favorites.

The Great Escape

Let me tell you a hamster tale — uh, tail? It's true and is about my friend Rachel. Rachel's family has lots of pets — cats and guinea pigs and praying mantises. But you know they are really smart people, because they have hamsters, too!

Rachel had two Chinese Dwarf hamsters. A week after bringing them home, Rachel found that one of her hamsters — the one named Rosie — was missing. After looking and looking, Rachel couldn't find Rosie and worried that one of the cats had eaten her. (This is the really sad part of the story. But don't worry, it gets better!)

A long, long time later — about six months — Rachel's dad was looking in the cupboard in Rachel's bedroom. He thought he heard a squeak from inside an ice skate. Squeaking skates? He looked into the skate, and there was Rosie! The tiny hamster had made a nice home for herself in the skate. She was healthy, with a cosy

nest and a very big stash of food. Where did all the food come from? Rachel thinks that every night Rosie waited until everybody was asleep. Then she ran to the hamster cage to collect any food that had spilled over!

Rosie is now living in her cage instead of the skate, and she doesn't have to sneak out to get her food.

My Hamster Notebook

This is the best story about me and my pet hamster:

_____

_____

_____

_____

_____

_____

_____

**Cheeky hamster Tumbleweed™ is a star host
of TVOntario's daily programming for kids.**

Catch the tvokids daily in The Nook or The Crawlspace
or join them on-line anytime at www.tvokids.com.
For more information on Tumbleweed and
on TVO programming, visit www.tvokids.com.

Tumbleweed and tvokids are trademarks
of TVOntario, the broadcasting service of
The Ontario Educational Communications Authority.

Where education matters — on air, on-line.

tvokids   **TV**Ontario

Dedication

The day it was confirmed I would be writing this book I just happened to be visiting a friend and his young son Christopher. Christopher and his hamster Storm were kind enough to give me lots of invaluable advice about the whys and hows of hamster life. In fact, Storm was even kind enough to run up my sweater sleeve and disappear in the folds of my blouse just to show that he could! Many thanks to Christopher Allward and Storm. I'd also like to thank Erica, Jessy and Rachel McLean, the great kids from next door, who told me the true life story of Rosie, the hamster escape artist. Thanks guys. — L.T.

Text © 2002 Kids Can Press Ltd.
Illustrations © 2002 Jane Kurisu

Kids Can Press acknowledges the support of the Government of Canada, through the BPIDP, for our publishing activity.

Published in Canada by
Kids Can Press Ltd.
29 Birch Avenue
Toronto, ON M4V 1E2

Published in the U.S. by
Kids Can Press Ltd.
2250 Military Road
Tonawanda, NY 14150

www.kidscanpress.com

Edited by Kat Mototsune
Designed by Julia Naimska
Printed in Hong Kong, China, by Wing King Tong Co. Ltd.

CM PA 02 0 9 8 7 6 5 4 3 2 1

1-55337-099-6

Kids Can Press is a *corus*™ Entertainment company